THE FARM

THE FARM

A Love that Lives On

SANDRA WOLFRAM
and EMMA RIEDL

THE FARM
A LOVE THAT LIVES ON

iUniverse books may be ordered through booksellers or by contacting:

iUniverse
1663 Liberty Drive
Bloomington, IN 47403
www.iuniverse.com
844-349-9409

Because of the dynamic nature of the Internet, any web addresses or links contained in this book may have changed since publication and may no longer be valid. The views expressed in this work are solely those of the author and do not necessarily reflect the views of the publisher, and the publisher hereby disclaims any responsibility for them.

Any people depicted in stock imagery provided by Getty Images are models, and such images are being used for illustrative purposes only. Certain stock imagery © Getty Images.

ISBN: 978-1-6632-1599-4 (sc)
ISBN: 978-1-6632-1600-7 (e)

Library of Congress Control Number: 2021900487

Print information available on the last page.

iUniverse rev. date: 01/13/2021

Contents

I dedicate this book to my late husband, Duane E. Wolfram—a man with an amazing vision and who loved living it. And to my family, who made this all possible: my daughter, Rebecca, and her husband, Doug; the children, Emma, Anna, Matthew, and Claire. Without them, none of this would have been possible. A very special note of gratitude and love to Emma, who spent the summer of 2020 working with me on putting together this amazing memoir. Thank you, Emma! And to my other two granddaughters, Anna and Claire, who designed our cover: thank you both for your beautiful addition to this book.

Foreword

As two people fall in love, they start to share a life. From the very beginning of this book, you will read about love between two people, love for a family, and love that fueled a divine passion. As this book was taking shape, there was a choice to decide on what exactly this book should encompass. The story is not necessarily one that is very conventional. In fact, this story is about creating the life you want with persistence and, most importantly, love for all things life brings you.

I am Sandra's oldest granddaughter, Emma. Although Sandra, or Gigi to me, had expressed interest in sharing this story with people, it was not until years later that we made this a reality. I saw it as another opportunity that I was so fortunate to share in the beginning, but it turned out to be that and much more. She and I would find ourselves sitting in our current farmhouse kitchen area multiple times a week for hours at a time. Sandra would walk me through the property and tell me stories. There was always a theme to her stories, and two were very common: preservation and sharing. This passion that my grandma and grandpa shared was one that started between the two of them as a hobby, turned into a lifestyle, and was eventually shared with family and way more.

The farm holds a special place in all of our hearts. I find trying to describe or pinpoint the meaning of the farm one of the hardest to put into words, but it has been my life and an amazing one at that. I am confident that no matter where I am or at what point I am at in my own life, the farm will always be home. I am excited to share my grandmother's story on this piece of land in a rural town in Northwestern Illinois, where I and many others can find a sense of home.

History

When most families look for a weekend home, they often look for homes in warmer states or on the water or in the mountains. This was not the case for our story. My husband, Dewey Wolfram, and I had purchased a beautiful two-story farmhouse on a special piece of land. The property originally set for a country retreat turned into a preservation project and holds a beautiful antique collection. This story is not an easy one to tell because, besides every property having family history and so many of those stories, this one also has stories of the past, told through antiques and restored buildings.

Before the Oak Hill Farm entered our family, it had been owned by the McFaddens dating back to the mid 1800s. They owned three hundred acres of land, which was plenty of room to raise their family of ten children. They had five girls and five boys. The McFaddens had quite a variety of farm animals, including cows, chickens, horses, sheep, and pigs. It was a typical nineteenth- and twentieth-century old-fashioned farm with some tillable land used for crops such as corn and wheat. When they lived on the property, they lived in the farmhouse, where my daughter and her family currently live. The farmhouse has two staircases, the reason being that one was used for the girls to go upstairs and the other was used for the boys to go upstairs, as they were not allowed to use the same stairs. As the McFadden family grew old and had families of their own, there were two daughters and one son who had never married and lived in that farmhouse while they performed the farm's upkeep.

Eventually, they decided it was time to sell the farm. The three hundred acres were sold to Frank Gabel, who was married to Antonio Gabel, or Mrs. Gabel. Mrs. Gabel was strong and hardworking. She always had her hair pulled back to keep it out of her eyes while she worked, even on the day we first met her. In fact, she was such a determined lady that one day, her car would not start, and she needed to get to town for a hair appointment. That led her to walking into town, about three miles, for a haircut, leaving the car behind. Frank's children never lived on the farm. Only Mrs. Gabel's daughter did in a makeshift apartment in the upstairs of the farmhouse. Frank Gabel had several children before marrying Antonio. We heard stories that there was animosity in the family as they tried to decide if Mrs. Gabel had married Frank for financial motives. Mrs. Gabel wanted to prove to Mr. Gabel's children that this was not the case and purchased half the acreage from Mr. Gabel. This is one reason why we purchased 150 acres, because the other half was sold elsewhere. When Frank passed away, his half of the farm was left to thirteen relatives. When we wanted to purchase from Mrs. Gabel, we needed approval from all of those thirteen relatives.

The farm is located in rural Illinois in a small town called Apple River, in Jo Daviess County. This quaint town in the Northwestern Illinois county, which holds a lot of early Illinois history, is surrounded by beautiful rolling farmland and borders Wisconsin and the Mississippi River. It has about four hundred people living there and is about eight miles to the nearest town over, Warren. My husband, Dewey Wolfram, went to high school in Warren. He grew up on a farm outside town and worked there for the duration of his adolescent years. After his father passed away in 1961, the farm was sold, and his mother, Katherine, moved into a house in Warren. Dewey ended up leaving the area to attend college at Northwestern

University to study finance. Though he was determined to leave the rural area, he paid visits to his mother, which I eventually accompanied him on, not knowing that one day, the visits would not require such a long drive.

A Love Affair

I grew up in Rochester, Minnesota, and eventually continued my education there to pursue a teaching career. In 1963, my last year of college at the University of Minnesota, during my student teaching, I met a man. His name was Duane Wolfram, but he also went by Dewey. The first time Dewey and I met, we were at an apartment party at my university. He had already an established insurance career in Chicago when he was sent to Minnesota to open up a new office for his company. He came with his friends, and I came with mine.

Dewey was very confident, fun, and well—how do I say it?—he just had this personality that drew you to him. Although at times he could be a little cocky—my grandson reminds me of him a lot—he joked around and carried himself with a purpose, which I admired. I remember that night when he and I sat and talked by the apartment pool for a couple of hours. Immediately, I could tell that he was a man of substance. Two days later, he was supposed to return to Chicago for a business meeting, and he invited me to go back with him. I declined so that I could keep teaching in Minneapolis. Dewey was actually working in that Minnesota office for two years, during which we dated for the duration.

Early in the spring of 1965, he had this plan to go back to Chicago permanently, and it really worried me, to be honest. He was seven years older than me, with three children from a previous marriage. Remember, at the time, I was twenty-three, and my family was not thrilled by the idea of it all. However, our relationship just seemed to work. Our idea of what we each wanted from life seemed to flow together flawlessly.

I know with great confidence God had put me in a place where Dewey and I would meet. That turned out to be the greatest love affair of my life. We married in August 1965 and had a wonderful life—that is such a phrase. But we did have a wonderful life. We were very much alike in many ways and very different in many ways, so there was never a dull moment.

Dewey's work relocated back to Chicago in 1965, and this time I went with him. He continued in insurance, and I was teaching at a school walking distance from our apartment. Three years later, Dewey's three children, who had been living with their mother, came to live with us full time. Suddenly, a family of two turned into a family of five, all living in a condominium that was far too small. However, we made it work for two years. Then life happened, the way it always seems to do, and my daughter Rebecca Ann Wolfram was born in 1970. With that addition, the condominium was not working anymore. This prompted a move to the suburbs of Chicago. All six of us moved into a house in Palatine, a Northwestern residential suburb.

When Rebecca was born, we were thinking of looking for a place in the country that could be a getaway. It sounded like the perfect idea to have a home away from home that had a sense of calm. At that time, Apple Canyon Lake was being developed near Warren, IL. As I mentioned, Warren was where Dewey attended high school. Dewey and I decided to drive two and a half hours to see this manmade lake. Even though it would be a beautiful lake development, and it is now, we felt we wanted to look for more space.

About a year later, while visiting Katherine, we met an old friend of Dewey's. After discussing our quest with him, he said, "Perhaps you should drive out to the Gabel farm. She may be thinking of selling." We asked for the directions and decided that we would go the next day.

Stubborn Determination

Dewey and I turned off of Stagecoach Trail, wondering where the road was going. There was not a sight of the house at the time. For about a mile until the farm, there was only wooded land on either side of the road. In fact, I remember how beautiful it was. Once farmers started buying the land along our driveway and chopping trees, it changed the drive up to the house completely, and it was just sad.

It seemed that the mysterious driveway was a part of the attraction. As we drove up the hill, I could see a two-tone pink farmhouse, which was in dire need of another pink coat of paint. Junk cars, weeds, and what seemed to be so many fences filled the property. The concrete was cracked. It just looked like a junkyard but somehow, I thought it was beautiful. It is hard to describe, but it was a mess. As bad as it appeared, in my head, I just knew, "This has got to be the place." Taking in the landscape of this farmland, my heart was saying, "This is the perfect place." Set far back off a major road, traditional farm buildings, fenced-in pastures, an old windmill—it was perfect. I wondered what Dewey was thinking, but I was too afraid to ask.

When we met Mrs. Antonio Gabel and introduced ourselves, she was not impressed that we had driven up unannounced. After a brief explanation of the purpose of our visit, she promptly replied, "The farm is not for sale." My husband said he would like to stay in touch, which I thought was pointless, but Dewey always seemed to know what to say.

As we drove away, Dewey said, "I could see us here. This is a great piece of property, but it needs a lot of work."

I was so happy to hear that, I could not even reply.

We did not talk about the farm much after that. It seemed there was no possibility of obtaining it. Approximately six months later, in the fall, Dewey thought it might be a good idea to visit Mrs. Gabel again. Dewey was a stubborn, determined man with a German will. This visit was a bit more encouraging.

Mrs. Gabel talked about possibly listing the property in the spring. She had lived in the Chicago suburbs before moving to marry Frank Gabel. She was planning to put an ad in *The Chicago Tribune* to attract Chicago buyers. That was not good news to us, as we were hoping to keep it all to ourselves. We wanted to stay low key but still in the game.

All through this process, I had asked the Lord to make it possible for us to be on that farm someday. I prayed and asked, "If it be Your will." Sometimes I really wanted to tell God what that will should be!

It is the spring of 1972, the farm was now for sale at a price that was far higher than farmland was going for. This was not a farm for actual farming. It was mostly woods and pastures, with very little tillable land. Due to the inflated price, we did not make an offer. We were both feeling defeated but realized that it was her right to do what she felt she needed to do.

I stepped out of the picture, but Dewey occasionally called her to get updates. He even went to see her early that summer to get a feel for what was happening. I continued to pray that somehow it would all work out. One of the prayers I would say was a promise to God that I would share the farm with everyone. At the time, I was thinking of celebrations of Christmas and Thanksgiving and family gatherings. Little did I know what everyone really meant!

We had a hot summer in July 1972. I remember I was ironing when Dewey called me to tell me the news. Antonio Gabel had sold the farm to a party in Hazel Green for $750 an acre. I will never forget the sadness that rolled over me, hearing that news. The bottom line was that we needed to accept the fact and go on. It was over.

It appeared God's will be that the farm should not be ours.

> Now Glory be to God who by his mighty
> power at work within us is able to do far
> more than we would ever ask or dream of.
> —Ephesians 3:20

That fall, it happened. Mrs. Gabel called Dewey at the office and said the sale had fallen through. "It did not work out. Do you want to talk?" Dewey hopped in the car that day and settled on terms that were fair and equitable.

As the closing papers were being drawn up, we found out that Mrs. Gabel owned only half of the farm. This meant that the other half of the farm belonged to thirteen relatives of Mr. Gabel. We would need permission from all thirteen relatives before we could own this farm, our dream.

Two of the thirteen relatives did not agree to sell the farm because they thought it was worth more per acre. Everything hung on these two individuals, who appeared to have control of this transaction. Eventually, they were finally able to come to terms and sell the farm, after many discussions with the parties and our attorney. Every day, I waited for a call to tell us it was resolved. Finally, there was agreement, and we closed in February 1973, in the middle of a blizzard.

During this time, I became a stay-at-home mom, and Dewey's career tremendously helped make that possible for our family. Dewey had an insurance business, and he invited me to work with him in 1975. Dewey was the general agent, and I did a lot of the training (due to my background in education), along with my own personal selling of insurance. This partnership worked out well, and it continues with the client base I still have.

The Hobby Out of Control

When you buy a piece of property and have a vision, there is a preservation and restoration process. It requires time and effort by everyone as the vision is being brought to life. Dewey, his kids (Blair, Brooke, Lea, and our daughter Rebecca) and I dedicated so much time on that farm in the beginning years. With numerous projects taking place, our weekend trips to the farm were a lot less relaxing than we would have thought. Dinner was always after mowing, trimming, and daily chores. We loved the work. It was our life, and our perfect life it was.

Dewey and I devoted our weekends to that farm. Every Friday, we would drive up that wooded lane, knowing there was work ahead, but that never bothered us. In fact, we had a furry greeter on four legs that sat at the base of our driveway every Friday. Her name was Mitsy, Mrs. Gabel's old dog, who was so loyal to that land. When Mrs. Gabel left for Arizona, she found Mitsy a home with a family at Apple Canyon Lake. On one of our first visits to the farm, we found Mitsy waiting for us with a torn leg from a fence she crawled under after traveling at least eight miles back to the farm. From then on, we made sure RJ Spillane, a dear friend who helped with many of our projects, fed her while we were away. That was her home first, and we were to share it with her.

Between 1974 and 1975, we had two main projects: a pond and a path of pine trees. The path of pines developed as a project after Dewey and I fell in love with the beautiful trees on our drive up to the property in the very beginning. We then bought twenty-five baby trees from the University of Illinois Extension Office for twenty-five cents apiece. The path of pines also served as a windbreak from the house. The wind would come from the west, and without a wind block, the farmhouse took the brunt of the power. Now there is a metal shed that is an additional wind block, but we still enjoy the big, beautiful trees in the backyard of the farmhouse.

In terms of the pond, that was one of Dewey's main visions from the start. He always wanted one on the farm, so we hired a crew to come one weekend to dig it up with their bulldozers and equipment. It is important to note that the farm is around twenty miles from a town rich in history, Galena. The reason Galena exists is because of the lead mines back in the day. Galena is close to the Mississippi River, so it was easy to transport the locally mined lead out of the area. In fact, the word "Galena" actually means "lead."

So, when the contractors for the pond came with their bulldozers, they struck a streak of lead. They came to the exciting conclusion that the area was an old lead mine. After going to get different equipment better prepared for a possible lead mine, they wanted to make a deal with Dewey that if they struck lead, they would get half of the proceeds. Dewey agreed, and there was even a written agreement everyone signed. Now there was a chance everyone could be rich! However, a few feet lower, the contractors struck water. The small amount of lead they found originally now remains in one of the big wooden barns on the property.

After the pond was dug, we stocked the pond with fish and added a floating raft. It was tied up, but we often took lawn chairs and floated on it in the middle of the pond. During the cold day in winters, we would all go and ice skate on the pond. However, it often leaked, which did not thrill me, as I wanted to spend money on wallpaper removal in the farmhouse rather than a leaking pond. Sometimes I hated that pond, but it is beautiful and is still used today by my grandchildren.

The Farmhouse

Taking one project at a time, we made additions to the Gabel farmhouse. Built in 1876, the farmhouse was unique. The kitchen was small, adjoined by a decent-sized dining area. On the main floor, there was a bedroom directly off the living room. There were two doors going into the bedroom, one at each end of the room. The bedroom had originally been a master bedroom with a nursery attached. When we purchased the farm, the room had been renovated into one large bedroom, but you could tell where the wall had been that divided it. There was a nice-sized living room with four big windows that let in so much light from the south and the west.

Upstairs, there were seven bedrooms. They had to have been small but had since been redone into four rooms. Again, you could tell where the original walls had been. There were the two staircases going up, one for the girls and one for the boys. And there was a wall that divided the upstairs completely. Over the years, we have made changes by adding bathrooms and updating the rooms, but they do still exude the history.

Perhaps the most memorable thing about the house was the wallpaper. Every wall and ceiling was covered with bold, bright flowered paper. We were told that Mrs. Gabel had put it all up herself. Eventually, I was able to make changes, but I kept a little sample of all the different patterns.

Over the years from 1973 to the 80s, we were able to cope with the house as it was. However, more room would have been welcomed. So, in 1984, we added a family room with a porch and a garage underneath. My husband was a planner and had some very definite ideas about the room. We had purchased a regulation-size pool table at an auction and knew we needed room for that.

Then we were blessed with an idea from a friend who told us about an old log cabin that was going to be taken down. He encouraged us to take the entire cabin and rebuild it at the farm. We opted to take a portion and reinstall it in the new room as one wall. Jim Thompson and his crew took it down, marked the logs, and carefully put it back inside the new room. The rest of the walls were barn wood that we had saved from taking down an old barn on another property.

We wanted a fireplace, and it turned out one could be created from bricks from the streets of Warren. There is more about this when you meet Scott. The room turned out to be just perfect—lots of space, a garage, a porch, and a fireplace.

Fast-forward a few years, and we discussed the idea of another addition. This would be an office. As we looked ahead, we could see continuing to work not only in our Chicago office but also from the farm. Our goal was to retire to the farmhouse, and an office would be a welcome addition.

In 1993, the office addition was built on to the west side of the house. We made the door entering the new room extra-large and obtained a pocket door from a salvage yard in Chicago. This made it seem less like an addition. We were also happy to find a beautiful old oak mantle to adorn the fireplace in the room. Our goal was to make it a comfortable room, not like an office. I feel we succeeded, as it is very cozy and yet very useful! The farmhouse has been home to my daughter and her husband and four children. Many decorating ideas and some updating have made it very warm and welcoming.

As we came out from Chicago every weekend and developed an attraction to attending auctions, it was clear that between the two of us and the kids, Dewey and I could not keep up the mowing of the lawn and other details while running all over Jo Daviess County and Southern Wisconsin. One Friday evening, while scouring the paper for auctions, Dewey came upon an advertisement from a thirteen-year-old boy named Scott Byrne that read, "I will mow lawns. I have my own mower."

He said to me, "This is what we need!"

The next morning, I called the number and talked to Scott's mother, who immediately agreed to have Scott ready to be picked up that afternoon. Scott later told me that when his mother announced that a lady from a nearby farm was going to pick him up, he was frightened. He was so young, so going somewhere with a stranger was not exactly what he was expecting when he put the ad in the paper. However, we got along right from the start.

We had a riding mower for him to use, even though he said he had his own, and he adapted to it in no time. The areas around that farm that needed to be mowed were done quickly. It was obvious this young man knew how to work. He and his older brother had worked on many farms during the summers and had loaded hay bales during harvest. That is hard work! He was anxious to work with us on weekends even though he had thirteen other mowing jobs around the town of Apple River!

There were multiple fences on the property as Mrs. Gabel had penned in some small animals. We wanted them down, so Dewey and Scott spent hours removing them. This gave them plenty of time to get to know each other and discuss many topics. As projects popped up, it was natural to call Scott to assist, and it was even better once he got his driver's license.

As many kids in this area were heavily involved in the community, Scott was also involved in sports throughout high school. He played in the band and continued to spend time at the farm. He was involved with so many of the projects we got into. He even got all dressed up and helped out at a dinner party. He looked distinguished in his purple silk shirt.

When we were talking about all the years that he had spent with us, he said the most memorable event was a Saturday morning, when Dewey said, "Come early. We are going to Warren." Scott had asked Dewey what they were going to do, and he replied, "You'll find out," with that familiar little smirk on Dewey's face. They hooked up a trailer, and Dewey had two strange-looking pieces of equipment with him. When Scott asked him what they were, he replied, "You'll find out," with a twinkle in his eye.

It is important to provide a little background on the project that these two started. The streets in Warren had been old brick streets. However, the village had taken them up and paved Main Street. The bricks were all piled up outside of town and were free for the taking. Scott found out that the odd pieces of equipment were brick carriers and each could hold five bricks. Yes, the work that day would be long, since Dewey had this image of putting them in our farmhouse.

That day, they loaded five hundred bricks onto the trailer and then unloaded them at the farm. The bricks are now a patio and sidewalk outside the farmhouse and surround a beautiful fireplace as well.

Over the years, Scott had a hand in setting up the country store, painting the schoolhouse and several barns. He also helped Jim Thompson on the renovation of the barn house by removing stanchions in what is now the kitchen.

Later, in 2000, he married his wife, Melissa, and is now father to three children. All these changes did not change his life as far as the farm went. He has been my right hand for thirty-four years now. We laugh about how we call Scott if we can't find something and he will pinpoint where it is. He keeps our storage room in the shed in perfect order. He is a master at getting our Christmas decorations ready for the holidays and packing them up afterward. Most of my friends want a Scott in their life. I am so blessed that he has been in mine for as long as he has.

Summer Kitchen 1985

When the farmhouse was built in 1876, a summer kitchen was constructed to the west of the house. A summer kitchen's primary purpose back in the day was to cook and can vegetables and fruit in the hot weather to keep the heat out of the house. They also did laundry and ironing there. When we purchased the farm, the summer kitchen had been turned into a one-car garage. Mrs. Gabel had installed a garage door on the south end and removed one large cupboard to enable a vehicle to enter.

After it became a garage, only the original walls and one large cupboard remained. At first, we used it to park a lawnmower and hang tools since there was no garage on the premises. It was very convenient being so close to the house. Fortunately, a relative of the McFaddens gave us some pictures that showed the original layout of the summer kitchen. They were invaluable once we started to restore the building to its original use because it helped me understand what the walls and interior set-up looked like.

As mentioned before, in 1984, we added a family room onto the farmhouse with a garage below. Since we now had a garage with a tool bench and storage for mowers, we thought it would be fun to restore the summer kitchen to its original state. Jim Thompson and his crew removed the garage door, rebuilt the wall, and added a door leading out to a patio area. Now we had a whole new purpose in going to auctions.

A summer kitchen would not have had a ceiling, as the purpose was to let the heat rise, but we wanted to display the many utensils we had collected. Luckily, we found a small amount of tin from a ceiling, and Jim installed it. The oak kitchen cupboard belonged to my grandmother in Minnesota. It never quite fit in anywhere but found its perfect place in the summer kitchen. The old dry sink with shelves was found in an old building at an auction near Winslow, Illinois.

It was fairly easy to find old kitchen utensils and items that fit into the summer kitchen. The butcher's block came from an auction near Scales Mound, IL, and took six men to move it. The most difficult item to find was the wood cookstove. If we did find one, it was usually all rusty and in bad condition. Eventually, a friend from Rockford who knew we were looking saw a great stove in an antique shop there.

I traveled to see it, and it was perfect. For $800, the stove was ours, and they delivered it! After we got it installed and piped correctly, we have enjoyed cooking out there on holidays and having Tom and Jerry's at Christmas.

On the north side of the summer kitchen, there is a quaint old wooden building that has been on the farm since the beginning.

Standing at about twenty feet tall and stored to the top with wood, the building's entire floor was covered with dirt. Two areas on the wall swing out for ventilation along with a window to the east. The door where one would enter was only five feet tall, which added some character to it.

After cleaning out the wooden building, it had been used for odds and ends. It did still serve its main use to supply the summer kitchen stove with wood as well as the wood-burning stoves in the farmhouse. Though there were no fireplaces in the farmhouse when we moved in, Dewey wanted to add one that would be big enough to put a kettle in. The fireplace was to be made of bricks from the streets of Warren that he and Scott had picked up and stored. Very often, while we were back in Chicago from Monday through Friday, it was common for contractors to work on projects during the week. This was the case with the brick masons building the fireplace. One Friday night, we came out to a finished fireplace. Oh, Dewey was so upset! The brick he and Scott collected was gorgeous but not nearly the size he wanted. It was also too late to fix, a chimney had been added to the house. The size was permanent, and Dewey learned to deal with it.

Back to the beloved old woodshed, in 2019, it would be changed. It was to become the woodshed bar and incorporated into wedding receptions. The dirt floor was covered with tile, and a window that opened inward for serving guests was installed on the north wall. A few shelves were put up, and several beer signs collected over the years were hung along with items from the Potosi

Brewing Company, which we bought at an auction in the 70s. These antiques would finally have a home to be admired by all. Just recently, we found a 1936 General-Electric refrigerator that actually works. That completed our woodshed bar.

The Country Store

All throughout the 1970s and 80s, we managed to get to an auction almost every weekend. When we arrived at the farm on Friday night, Dewey would scour the local papers for sales, a paper in one hand and a scotch on the rocks in the other. Our weekend plans would then center on the location and time of the sale we wanted to be at. Sometimes we would split up so we could cover more than one. His main interest was the horse-drawn machinery and tools, and I was looking at furniture and all the old wonderful kitchen items, plus old vintage clothing that I loved.

Every time we would attend an auction and purchase an antique, there was a story to go with it. I could walk around the property today and still tell stories about where it had been purchased or who had owned it before we did.

At many auctions, you may find one piece that you are interested in but it comes in a box with ten additional pieces. So, if I wanted one plate, I might have to buy the matching set of cups and silverware to go with it. Perhaps this is how the collection grew so quickly.

Often, we would attend a sale on Sunday, bring our loot back to the farm, stash it in the big barn, and get ready to go back to the city. There were also multiple times that we did not even have time to look in detail into the boxes of goodies that we had purchased. Eventually, we sorted through the different antiques and set up a display in the big barn, although very temporary and rough.

North of the big barn is a building that had two distinct uses. One side is a granary, a storage space for grain. The other side was a shed used for small machine repairs. Toward the back of the building, there was a shelf with tools and equipment. Since I am not trying to repair small machines, I immediately had a vision to store my antiques here. Saying that I wanted to store them is an understatement. I wanted to display my antiques and treasures. There was just one problem: I had no shelves or cabinets to do so.

Lo and behold, we read about a hardware store in Galena called the Milhouse Lumber Company. They were closing their doors and selling everything, right down to the shelving on the walls. This looked and sounded promising. The day of that sale, Dewey had another auction he was interested in attending, so off to Galena I went, all by myself. It was long and boring at first, as they sold paint, nails, tools, and other such hardware items. Finally, the shelves that lined the walls of the narrow old building were going to be auctioned. I bid on one section of fifteen feet and got it for thirty-five dollars. Wow, I was happy! At that point, it did not bother me that it was quite permanently attached to the wall of the building.

Most people had left the sale by now when the auctioneer said there were a few things on the third floor. About thirty-five of us followed him upstairs to find a beautiful old shelving unit from the original store plan. It was long and tall and perfect.

No other person had any interest, so I purchased it for fifty dollars. What a thrill it was to find beautiful pieces you never expected to see. Again, the one small detail I had neglected to pay attention to was the stipulation that all this had to be removed by the following Saturday. All the way home, I was thinking of how I was going to break this fabulous news to Dewey, at the same time telling him the timeframe involved with retrieving all the pieces, which came in large sizes. Without going into detail, the initial reaction on his part was not pleasant.

Luckily, Dewey and I had a week to get a crew together to help. This was in the dead of winter, and we had a long snowmobile trailer that we thought would do the trick to haul the pieces home. On the following Saturday morning, we were off to pick things up. It was Dewey's first time seeing the shelving unit, and he might not have been as happy as I was with the size of it. Getting the large shelving unit down from the third floor almost proved to be a cause for divorce. However, we endured, and it was loaded on the trailer. The other unit was not quite so bad, as it was on the main floor and came off the wall easily.

Over the next few months, we slowly got things set up on the side of the building that was used for small machines. Currently, there are two glass cases, similar to ones you might see in a jewelry store, that hold many small and fragile antiques. I mentioned that I grew up in Minnesota. My grandfather and his brother had a general store in Roscoe Center called the Peterson Brothers Store. When the store closed, I was fortunate to get the jewelry display case and the postal sorting cubby, and it is in our country store now.

There is a huge beautiful oak counter that is now at the back of our country store. It holds an antique scale and a cash register. This really started to look like a replica of an older country store after purchasing the counter in Council Hill, a Wisconsin town fifteen miles from the farm. It was beautiful but had more of a bohemian aesthetic than I wanted for our antique building. Originally, it was painted bright lime green, but I could see it stripped down to the original oak. We bought it and fixed it up. The refinishing proved true—it is beautiful.

Echoes of the Past

As additions and renovations were slowly being made to the farm, I really found a joy in sharing the property. Dewey found quite a hobby as well. Soon, my husband became aware that horse-drawn machinery from early farming days was quite prevalent at these auctions. Before long, he had quite a collection consisting of corn pickers, a rare hay baler, plows of all kinds, planters, and threshing machines, to name a few. Having a farm background, he understood all their roles in the farming process and organized them in order in one of our large barns in the back of the farm.

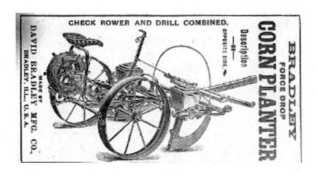

Dewey acquired quite the collection of early 1900s farm machinery, and he had found that many of his friends in the area shared this interest in historical farming. We had tillable land to use, and Dewey was excited to use this machinery on it. However, we had no horses at that time. So, a few of Dewey's friends brought horses to the farm, and they all started hitching their horses to the machinery. The men were like a couple of kids playing with some of the old machinery.

As Dewey formed a core group to share this hobby with, more men wanted to bring horses and machinery as word traveled. Soon the men brought the wives and children and made a weekend during harvest time to come and use the old farm machinery.

One year, an idea took place to host an event over Labor Day weekend, which seemed logical with an extra day, making it a three-day weekend. Dewey and I would open our home to those who wanted to come out and watch the horse-drawn farm machinery demonstrations take place. The schoolhouse and buildings would be open for tours, our Model A and other antiques would be out for display, and people could spend as much time as they liked enjoying the farm.

After hosting this event for a few years consistently, it became an annual event, with more and more participation using more and more of the equipment. People from surrounding communities came to watch the activities. Wives of the men participating started making lunch for the spectators, and at one point, there were over three hundred people that passed through the farm enjoying the demonstrations over the three-day weekend! This was definitely an example of how my expression about sharing the farm with everyone was a reality.

The name Echoes of the Past became attached to the annual event. Connie Spillane, RJ's daughter, came up with the name. Boy, I loved it right away.

This event took place for twenty-six years; it went from a hobby with my husband to a weekend that my grandchildren eventually were able to attend and enjoy as well.

The event continued for a few years after Dewey's death but gradually faded out. In 2013, we had an auction, so the collection was sold to Amish families who would use the pieces, and some went to a museum in Montana. It wasn't easy to see it go, but it was the best decision. The event had grown, and it became quite the production. Although it was so joyous to see so many people out enjoying what had been our dream, it was time for Echoes of the Past to dwindle out. I kept a few of the items, as they are close to my heart, that we can handle and demonstrate.

Not related to Echoes of the Past, but another group event that was enjoyed over the years was the Annual Office Picnic. Each summer, we set aside a weekend and invited all the folks involved with the insurance office to bring their families and enjoy the country. I believe in the saying "A day in the country is worth a month in town." Over the weekend, we had pony rides for the kids, hula-hoop contests, fishing in the Apple River, and wonderful food and beverage. Some pitched tents, and some slept under the stars. Part of the plan was to present awards to those deserving of top salesperson and others. The top salesperson received a genuine pair of Lee Bib Overalls, to be worn at the next year's picnic. There are so many wonderful memories of those weekends.

The School House 1991

In 1991, I was to turn fifty. I thought it was going to be another weekend spent with friends and those who came to the Echoes of the Past event each year. It was about four in the afternoon, and the plowing demonstrations had just ended. Dewey entered the house, and he told me that he had to show me something in our red shed at the back of our property. As I went back with him, it seemed he had been hiding all these people for a surprise fiftieth birthday party! As people arrived, the Echoes of the Past activities slowed, and I was suddenly the center of attention. What a shock! This was not like my husband; he was the master of delegation, but on this day, he had thrown together a celebration like no other.

A good time was had by all with a delicious buffet and music and dancing.

Throughout the night, friends were laughing and catching up. I remember that Dewey, at one point in the night, told me the biggest surprise yet. Dewey did not make an announcement. He told me when it was just the two of us. The gift was that we were going to add an old original one-room schoolhouse, which we were to find together, to our property.

Oh, I was surprised. I remember thinking, *Wow, what a journey we are about to go on to accomplish this.* There were so many schoolhouses that we had seen in the past that were so far gone that we did not know how we would restore one for us. I was at a loss for words, as this was a challenge but one of the most exciting.

As I mentioned, Dewey grew up on a farm outside Warren. He attended a one-room schoolhouse called Pucket School from first grade through eighth grade. He told numerous stories of the many teachers that had been hired and the trials some of them had with some pretty rough kids. Finally, a male teacher was hired and was able to get things in order. The stories reminded me of *Little House on the Prairie* episodes. Back in Minnesota, my mother taught in a one-room schoolhouse for a few years, so we both had fond memories of these buildings.

So, as we traveled through the countryside to our many auctions, we kept our eye out for old schoolhouses with the potential to be restored. Most were way too far gone to consider, but we did come upon one near Shullsburg, Wisconsin, that looked like a possibility. After some research, we located the owner and paid a visit. Mrs. Thompson was the owner, an older woman who had acquired the schoolhouse when it closed in 1939. It had been transformed into a hired man's house, a sheep barn, and then a feed storage building. It was rough, with a hole in the ceiling, creating a major problem with the floor. The entire roof seemed to be in bad shape.

Despite all this, she did not want to let it go. We explained to her that our intention was to move it and restore it, but the answer was no. She was sure she needed it for her feed bags. To make a long story short, we contacted her again over time, and she was finally convinced it might be nice to see the schoolhouse preserved. We bought it for $200. We now owned Monticello School, named for Monticello Township in Wisconsin. Now we had to plan to move it to the farm.

Into the picture comes the help of Bob (RJ) Spillane, a man capable of almost anything. RJ had lived in this area his whole life. He was truly a jack of all trades, as a farmer, road commissioner, husband, and one of the most well-known men in the community. You will find him in many places throughout the book. With his help, we moved the building on a big flatbed trailer after removing the roof, which was in bad shape. The first step was to decide where it would be placed on the farm. After much consideration, it was placed on a cement foundation near a grove of walnut trees that Dewey and I had planted. It was just far enough away from the farmhouse but close enough to admire from our porch. Jim Thompson and his crew did the renovation and restoration.

As you have noticed, Jim Thompson's name comes up frequently. Thompson Builders, a company from Warren, IL, has been amazing. A small group of talented and dedicated men have transformed things without a hitch. No matter what the project was, they were on it and seemed to enjoy most of the unusual projects. We have been so blessed to have a man like Jim and his crew work on the farm and lend their creativity to the restoration.

Jim Thompson had found wainscoting to match what was missing on the walls, put on a new ceiling and roof, repaired the siding, and built a bell tower. His father had once remodeled the high school in Warren. At that time, the blackboards were removed and replaced with the new whiteboards. Jim knew where the blackboards were stashed and brought them to our school. What a blessing to have those old beautiful blackboards!

In the meantime, Dewey and I were on the hunt for anything we might need, such as desks and books. Auctions provided many of these items, and as people heard what we were doing, they brought items and gave them to us.

When a school closed, it was common for the last teacher there to be allowed to take anything he or she wanted. My aunt as well as my mother taught in a one-room schoolhouse in West Concord, Minnesota. When that school closed, she took the teacher's desk and the picture of Lincoln and Washington home to her farmhouse. Upon learning of our restoration project, she offered the desk and the pictures to us. That was a wonderful beginning to furnishing the building.

Once the job was complete, we planned a party to celebrate and wanted to include anyone who had any connection with Monticello School. Dewey was researching to find individuals who might have attended the school and was fortunate to come up with some. So, in addition to all those invited, our honored guests were former teachers and classmates. One of the teachers brought pictures of children they had taught and old photos of activities.

The last teacher that had been at Monticello School was Shirley Franzen, from Apple River. She had taken the teacher's chair home in 1939. The day of the reunion, she brought the chair and returned it to the school.

It was a grand event. The gift had been fulfilled.

Two New Metal Barns

When we purchased the farm, there were six barns plus the little woodshed. As Dewey's collection of horse-drawn machinery grew, the large old barn to the south was filling up. He wanted to keep each piece covered, and many of the items were large—for example, the old Case threshing machine and the McCormick-Deering corn picker.

By 1978, it was apparent that he needed more space. None of the other buildings would be suitable, so he explored the idea of building a large new shed. He settled on a 50 × 80 metal Wick building, to be placed close to the original wooden barn. The construction started in September and was all done before winter set in. I had a feeling it wouldn't be too long before some treasure from an auction would find its new home in that shed.

The years went by, and both of the existing barns were almost a museum of the original plows, planters, and hay balers. There were now also a few buggies and items that Dewey felt should be more protected. That meant a cement floor and a way to make sure it was animal proof. The 1978 building had a gravel floor, and somehow, raccoons and other varmints found a way in. Thus, we needed a plan for an upscale building with ceiling lights and wall fixtures.

Construction began again in September 1995. We called this barn the "Anniversary Barn" as it went up. Why? We had our thirtieth wedding anniversary in August of that year.

We never did big things for our anniversary; however, I wanted to take a cruise for this one. I knew from the start that it would not be an idea that excited my husband. I thought he might agree, so I brought it up to him. Being the salesman he was, he convinced me that a new, beautiful red building with lights would give us more joy than pictures from a ship! Actually, he was right. That building has been one of the most valuable buildings on the property. It is now the center of wedding-day preparations and storage of numerous items.

Unfortunately, in October, Dewey became very ill and was diagnosed with lung cancer. He was quite weak through the fall months. However, all the people involved in the Echoes of the Past group, which had been going on for several years, came and moved the items that Dewey wanted into the newly finished building. He was able to direct them and participate in the setup. It was quite an emotional couple of days. He knew things were where he wanted them before his time on the farm became limited. I am so glad we built the building and did not go on a cruise!

A Tough Year

As I look back on all the years of projects and fun—holidays with family, visitors on weekends, auctions and moving buildings—1995 was a very tough year.

Dewey's youngest daughter, Brooke, had been ill for over four years and passed away in April, at age thirty-three. It was hard on everyone but particularly difficult for Dewey. She was a very sweet person. She was single and had lived with us for a few months. She and her dad had gotten very close during this time.

Going through the grieving process, time was not on our side, as Dewey was diagnosed with lung cancer in October 1995. This was a huge shock. He was a strong, healthy man and had gone through a routine annual physical in September with no indication that anything was wrong. That physical did not include a chest X-ray, and nothing showed up in any other tests. There are no words to describe the desperate feeling I had when he was admitted to Northwestern Hospital. He had become ill while we were at the farm. It was Sunday morning, and he wanted one thing—to get to Northwestern so he could see his good friend and doctor, Nadim Khoury.

The news was not good. It was stage-four cancer. Through the fall, the treatments were pretty tough on him. In December, the decision was made to stop all treatments, and he passed away on February 23, 1996. The funeral was in Apple River, and he was buried in a nearby cemetery. It was West Ella Cemetery, only a couple miles from the farm.

Proverb 16:9 says, "Man makes his plans, but the Lord directs his steps," had come to be very true in my life. The road ahead looked bleak.

Throughout the treatments Dewey had, he continued to go to the office as much as possible. We had an insurance/ investment business and had been working together for several years. He was the general agent, and I trained the salespeople as well as doing some selling myself. In January 1996, we started discussing what would become of the office, as he was aware at that time it was not going well for him. We contacted our major insurance carriers, and he requested they appoint me as general agent as of February 1, 1996.

At a family gathering around Christmas, we were fortunate to have a good night. It was such a meaningful night as Dewey gave a toast to announce that he was going to make me the first female general agent of the Guardian Life Insurance Company. Dewey toasted to a happy life that he was able to have and how proud he was to be passing down the title of general agent to me. This was when we all realized that he was really sick and had to make many decisions. It was such an intimate and special night with the family, one that we were all so lucky to get with Dewey.

That gave him some peace that things would go on smoothly. I remained in that position through April 1999, when I resigned, which I chose to do so I could spend more time at the farm.

I was going to the farm on weekends, as we had always done. However, it was much more difficult to be there alone than I thought it would be. I hoped that by being there more I could adjust to the emptiness. I kept thinking about how Dewey and I had said to one another, "When I die, I want to be buried on this farm." It was somewhat in jest but somehow serious, as we both loved the farm so much.

In April 1996, I decided to go to the Jo Daviess County Board and request a permit to move Dewey home to be buried at the farm. The idea was not received well. The board did not vote it down but tabled it for more information. One of the board members in favor of it visited me and threw out some ideas. We discussed how to prepare for the next month's meeting. He had known Dewey well and respected what we had done with the farm. He said, "Let me help you get this approved." He insisted that I invite the board members to visit here and point out where I might want this burial plot. The main issue with some members was the future of this gravesite. They were worried it would not be taken care of properly. They told me often, "You may take care of it, but what happens when you die is the concern." The board member that was working with me told me that I had to convince them that it would be tended to.

I appreciated his help and suggestions and did invite the board to visit. There were seventeen members on the board, and three of them accepted a little tour. To satisfy the concern of future care, my attorney suggested we draw up a trust so, at my death, my daughter, Rebecca, would be responsible. It passes on to family after that. Now I felt I was ready for the second meeting, which was a couple of weeks away.

One day, I received a phone call from a gentleman who wanted to talk about this permit. He said he had heard that I would get my burial permit if I had a church. That had never come up at all in any conversation. I told him that it was obviously a rumor. I almost laughed at the idea, but he was serious. He had attended a church that had closed in 1969 and was located on Elizabeth/Scales Mound Road. The parishioners that still lived nearby had tried to take care of it, but it was deteriorating. He said that since I needed a church, I could have their church. I was shocked; I knew of the exact church he was speaking of. My reaction was that I didn't need a church, and I dismissed the entire idea, thanking him for the thought.

The church he was referring to was St. John's Lutheran Church, built in 1860 in the township of Guilford. I did hear that someone had offered to buy it and make it a restaurant, but that was definitely not an option for the beautiful old building. I had driven by St. John's Church and knew the size of the building and was overwhelmed that anyone would even think of moving it. However, there was persistence in this group who had attended the church. I was contacted by more than one person after that, even though purchasing and moving a church was never on my agenda.

It seemed that the continued persistence worked, as owning a church was now a possibility in my mind. One of the parishioners that called me about St. John's Church referred me to Robert Childs. He and his sons had a moving business that specialized in moving large and unusual buildings. I decided to call him and explore the idea, thinking the church might not be able to be moved at all. Mr. Childs came down, and we went over to the location to examine the situation. He walked around the building, inspecting the old, worn foundation, and announced, "I can move her." I really hadn't expected that. We discussed some ballpark figures.

About that time, God's hand became more apparent in this plan. I received a call from an insurance company that Dewey had worked for years ago. The company had learned of his death and said there was some group life insurance still in force. If I sent in the proper forms, there would be a check in the mail that would cover the moving cost of the church. Was I supposed to be thinking that this should happen?

After working with Robert Childs and agreeing to his terms, we started to plan. This, of course, meant another permit. After much discussion with my family and others, such as RJ and Jim Thompson, we started thinking of where this church would go on the property. There would be more permits to obtain, and I really wondered what the county board would think now. It required drawings of where it would be placed and lots of details. I complied with their requests and obtained the permit to move the church. Summer was passing, and there was much to do at the location on Elizabeth/Scales Mound Road to prepare for this undertaking. While we were busy working with RJ Spillane on setting a foundation for St. John's and excavating around it for clearance, we were preparing a gravesite for Dewey's homecoming.

Let's reflect for a moment on moving Dewey from the cemetery to the farm. Since we were clear on doing this, we decided it would be appropriate to have the Labor Day Echoes of the Past event be an integral part of the ceremony. Everyone involved over the years agreed this was a perfect plan. The group wanted to bring the body home pulled by horses, and when the Herman Funeral Home found out, they offered an antique glass hearse to hold the coffin. When the hearse arrived, there was a ceremony on the farm to follow. Robert Dye, the pastor at Dewey's first funeral, attended to officiate this little ceremony. This included a reading from Doug Riedl, Rebecca's boyfriend at the time and my future son-in-law.

Toward the end of Dewey's life, Doug became closer with him. Dewey was not getting any healthier, and neither was his memory. At times, he was often confused and forgot what day it was. On Valentine's Day 1996, Dewey and Doug were upstairs as Rebecca and I were having a drink downstairs. Dewey had asked Doug what day it was, and after finding out it was Valentine's Day, he asked Doug to go get Valentines for Rebecca and myself.

It was the oddest occurrence, but Dewey signed Rebecca's valentine as Blue Moon. To this day, we do not know why. However, that story sticks with me, and it really meant a lot for Doug to be a part of the ceremony. Rebecca and I knew that Dewey trusted him a lot.

At the memorial service, Doug read "Persistence" by Calvin Coolidge. This was a reading I found in Dewey's desk when I was cleaning out his office. When I found this reading, I knew it spoke to who Dewey was and what he believed. It felt only right to have it be spoken at his homecoming. Doug was so nervous, as he will tell you to this day, but I thought he carried out that reading flawlessly.

Persistence
Calvin Coolidge

Nothing in the world can take the place of persistence.
Talent will not, nothing is more common than unsuccessful men with talent.
Genius will not: unrewarded genius is almost a proverb.
Education will not: the world is full of educated derelicts;
Persistence and determination alone are omnipotent;
The Slogan "Press on!" has solved and will solve the problems of the human race.

I sent out a letter to close friends and family letting them know our plan to move Dewey's grave to the farm. The word was out with neighbors and people from the surrounding area that this was going to occur. Suddenly, it was to be a huge homecoming party. That meant food and beverage and even music from a neighbor who did some DJ work now and then. The night ended with the song, "The Green Grass of Home." It was an old country song but quite appropriate for this day. Dewey was home at last.

The Church 1996

To prepare St. John's for the move, Robert Childs had been working almost three weeks at the original location. The actual village the church was closest to was Guilford, and the distance from the original location to the farm was fourteen miles. This was the distance we were going to have to move the church from one location to the next.

The date was set for September 18, 1996. The Jo Daviess county sheriff was notified, and a notice was put into local papers that Scales Mound Road and Stagecoach

Trail would be closed due to a church being moved. I often wonder what reactions people had to reading that. Before the moving of the church began, Commonwealth Edison had to be hired to accompany us taking down electrical wires in front of the truck and replacing them after.

At precisely 9:00 a.m., on the eighteenth of September, the truck pulled out of the original location and slowly started down the road. People had read about this, and many lined up along the road, watching the parade. We had a police escort in the front and in the back of the procession. The entire ordeal included the church on a huge flatbed, a pick-up truck full of spare tires, a vehicle with the rest of the Childs' moving crew, and our family in the back of a pickup truck for good viewing.

Stagecoach Trail is quite winding and very hilly. It was interesting to note that at times, the truck would get to almost thirty miles per hour going downhill in order to get up the hill again. This was a slow but memorable process.

Every now and then, Mr. Childs would stop and walk around the vehicle to examine the ropes and security of the building. It made me think of what he had said at the beginning of this whole plan. He said, "I want a third of the money before I touch the church, a third of it during the preparation, and the last third *if* I get her there." Now I knew there may have been a possibility of this church not making it to the farm, but everything was going well.

As the day progressed, we drew closer and closer to the farm. Not being able to come in the normal way on the lane due to trees, the truck turned on Hodgin Road, five miles west of the farm. It was a straight, narrow gravel road that led to the top of a hill just west of the site prepared. The final four miles of the trip was through cornfield waterways that our neighbor had mowed for us. What an amazing site to see this truck with a church coming through the field. The truck overheated at this point, so we sat and waited for it to cool down. Mr. Childs and our beloved St. John's Church arrived at the prepared foundation at exactly 6:00 p.m. that day.

The church was moved as you see it today, with the exception of the cross. Upon making the move, it was decided that the cross should come off, as it seemed to wobble a bit on a windy day and would definitely fall while being moved on a truck bed. The catch was how that would happen, as it was so very high. RJ Spillane to the rescue once again! That man could do and would do anything.

We hired Lyons Well Drilling Co. to bring their tall crane to the site. RJ had a fifty-gallon barrel that he attached to the crane. He got in the barrel, and Lyons lifted him to the cross. He easily lifted the cross out of its place and brought it down. It was very light, as it was hollow and finished with gold filigree.

RJ repeated the act of replacing the cross once the church arrived at the farm. He always joked that it was as close to heaven as he would ever get!

So many people had come to the farm to wait for the arrival of the church. It was such an amazing moment to have Dewey and a church all home after such memorable moves.

To the right of the St. John's Church, our Wolfram cemetery lies. As mentioned earlier, Dewey is buried there along with other family members and our dear friends, John and Melba Stark, who were like family. John was involved in many of our projects on the farm as he was the most talented electrician we knew. It is very fitting that they are a part of our Wolfram cemetery alongside Dewey.

The Wolfram Horse Barn 1997

During the restoration of the church, we were made aware that we would need old rock to put around the foundation. It was sitting on a cement base but definitely needed rock.

I knew that there were many barns in the area that were no longer used and were in rather bad shape. RJ told me that if I found a willing farmer, he would bulldoze the barn so we could take the rock and would clean up the site.

On that note, I started out on my journey to find rock.

When I spotted a barn that looked promising, meaning one in rough shape, I stopped and found someone and told my story. Most of the individuals just looked mystified and more or less shrugged me off. Most of the responses went something like this: "Oh, one day I might fix that old barn up" or "I think that barn needs to stay right where it is." Under every one of those barns was beautiful rock, even though I did not get it.

To have more credibility, I started taking a newspaper article that had been written about the church move, so I could prove my case and not appear to be nuts. That did not pan out either.

One day, I happened to drive south on Highway 78, where the old Wolfram Farm had been. It was now owned by a new couple that I knew. As I glanced over to the buildings, I realized one was exactly what I was looking for. Rather disheveled and in need of a new roof, I turned around and pulled in. Kathy, the farmer's wife, was at home, and I did not need to tell her the story about the church move, as she knew it well.

Upon asking her about the building, she replied that they were going to tear it down. That was the perfect answer. She agreed that we could take all the rock we wanted if we would get rid of the barn. Yippee!

I went right to RJ's and told him we were in business with old rock. He wanted to see the barn, so we returned to that farm where the barn was. Upon looking at the building, we realized it had been a horse barn back in the day.

Since Dewey's father had been that old-fashioned German farmer who never bought a tractor, there had always been a stalled barn for the workhorses. It was in rough shape. The floor was basically gone, and the wooden stalls all falling apart. RJ looked it over carefully. Then he looked at me and said, "We are not going to bulldoze this building. We are going to move it to the farm. We can restore this old girl." So, on that note, we restored yet another building: The Wolfram Horse Barn.

We found the barn in the fall and waited until the ground and roads were frozen so it could be moved easily on the backroads. RJ didn't want to bother with a permit or close any roads. He knew routes that we could take and not get caught. However, we did get caught. The road commissioner had a sense something was up. It did not help that he and RJ did not get along well (RJ had been the road commissioner for years before this!) So, he stopped us and told us we were out of bounds. There were words between RJ and the commissioner, and then I decided to speak up. This gentleman had gone to high school with Dewey. He knew about the church move, so I explained that we needed to move the barn to get the rock for the church foundation. I appealed to him to let us continue, and if there was a fine to pay, that was understandable.

He thought about it for a moment, and then he said it was all right for us to keep moving. He said as long as it was for "Peewee," which was Dewey's nickname in high school. So off we went. Thank you, Mr. Road Commissioner.

Over the winter, the barn was put back together, and restoration began. New stalls were built, and a cement floor was poured. In the process, we discovered a date and some initials painted into a board. The initials are JCW '85, which stands for John C. Wolfram, Dewey's grandfather. He built the barn back at that time. They are actually written *WJC '85*. Having that wonderful history in addition to the original horse weathervane was especially meaningful. The barn now is home to my son-in-law's draft horses, just as it was originally used!

A Time for Starting Over

T his memoir has a common theme that I really think
held deep importance in this part of my life—
preservation. As our hobby of attending auctions and
building our antique collection developed, our devotion
to preserving the use and history of each piece also
became extremely important. Projects started developing,
especially with our new building additions, as we kept
working on the farm. Preservation was the key to Dewey's
continuing determination and love for this farm. His
legacy is preserved, and it has always been important to
me to continue this even in the present day.

The church restoration was underway with Jim
Thompson at the helm, along with his crew. There was
far more to do than anyone expected. The walls were
crumbling from old plaster and had to be drywalled.
Fortunately, the floor was sound, and when the old carpet
was pulled up, there was a beautiful oak floor. The windows
were old, as the church was built in the 1860s, but all in
good shape. Since it came with all the pews and books and
the beautiful altar, much had to be moved out and stored as

the work was done. Fortunately, the bell in the bell tower made the trip safely and had a loud, meaningful sound when the rope was pulled.

The restoration started in late 1996. The goal was to have it completed by the spring of 1998. It actually went along better than expected and was done late 1997.

Rebecca and Doug were thinking of getting married in St. John's Church once restored, and the date was set for June 27, 1998. This would be a wonderful celebration and a new beginning. Plans were coming together for family members from all over to be present, and close friends were invited to participate in the ceremony. It was a joyous time to celebrate with so many friends and family members and share the farm with people, as I had always planned.

As I watched the team of horses pull the white carriage, my heart welled up with emotion. My husband and RJ had done so much together with teams of horses, and I knew he would have loved to have been a part of this. I so wished he could have walked his beautiful daughter down the aisle of that restored church. I knew that Rebecca would be feeling the same way. It was a very emotional, beautiful celebration overall.

Over the years from Dewey's death to the wedding, I had kept our residence in Park Ridge and had been going back and forth frequently. I was involved in my business and had clients near the farm and many in the Chicago area. I kept questioning whether I should continue that or sell the residence to simplify things. In August 1998, Becky and Doug came to me to announce two things: first, they were going to have a baby in the spring, and second, they were serious about moving to the farm to raise their children in the country. *Wow!* That was so exciting and so overwhelming! I was so excited about the thrill of a grandchild and the idea of living at the farm—so many emotions and possibilities and yet some concerns as to working out here. Both Becky and Doug had good jobs in the city that they had to orchestrate while wanting to make a huge life transition.

As we talked about it, they decided to put their home in Des Plaines, Illinois, on the market. I said to the Lord in my prayers one evening, "Well, God, if you think this is right, the house will sell, and if it isn't, then it will not for a long time. It is in your hands." The house sold in a few weeks. Congratulations and time to celebrate for all—now what?

The Barnhouse 1999

So now Becky and Doug had decided to follow the plan to live at the farm and raise their family in the country. I was elated.

Even though I had always yearned to live permanently at the farm, I had found the weekends to be very empty and difficult without Dewey. I was determined to make life at the farm work, so I was very happy I would not be all alone if this all worked out.

I had some second thoughts about their idea of moving out to such a rural area based on employment opportunities, which were slim, and the living arrangements for each of us. Though the farmhouse was spacious, I knew we could not all live together forever, especially if they wanted to raise a family there.

As I thought more about the move, and as we discussed it more and more, I tossed around the idea of building a home on the property. Yes, this time, the new project was building a structure instead of moving one on the back of a semi-truck to the farm. There were many places that would be desirable. However, there were so many buildings already. Did we need another roof?

This was on my mind quite often. Then the idea of possibly making our favorite barn into living quarters crossed my mind. The only way to know was to contact Jim Thompson.

This barn was directly across from the farmhouse and had been built in 1891. It was a large hay barn with milking quarters in the lower level. Even back in the late 1800s, twenty-six cows were milked there. Dewey and I had put a new roof on the building immediately after buying the farm. This definitely was a building we did not want to lose.

For many years, we stored many auction finds in that building and even set up a display of items and crocks in there before putting the country store together. One year, we cleaned it up quite nicely and had a barn dance party. It had already held so many fond memories.

Jim came out and examined the structure and the foundation in January 1999. I wanted to know if this was a possibility. His report was positive. The barn could be converted. I was prepared for a negative response since it had been built in 1891. I was so happy to know that it was possible!

Now that I had a confirmation from Jim Thompson, I needed to follow up with Doug and Becky. Their decision to get to the country was firm, and I announced to them that I had talked to Jim about converting the barn into my own barn house. They were horrified that I would live in a barn while they lived in the farmhouse. I assured them that I knew what I was doing and it would be fine.

I mean, I was working with Jim Thompson, so of course, everything would work itself out.

On April 18, 1999, Doug and Becky welcomed their first born, Emma Brooke. We were then all together in the farmhouse while the barnhouse project took place. This allowed me to have quality time with Emma when she was young, and it helped Doug and Becky, two new parents. In due time, I could move into the barn on one level while the work was being done.

Working with Jim is always a joy. He has creative ideas. Rather than have extensive blueprints, he sketches out those ideas as we discuss possibilities. We made decisions and then changed some of them as we went along with the project. After replacing some missing boards, black tar paper was wrapped around the entire outside of the building. Tyvek was next, then insulation, and finally, new barn wood. This process allowed the beautiful old barn wood to be preserved inside.

I mentioned the barn was built in 1891, but the lean-to addition, which became the garage, was an addition in the 1920s. To make use of that space, we removed a portion of the inside west wall. Then, using dormers, we converted the space into two bedrooms and an upstairs bath. I would never have dreamed that might be possible.

The main floor of the building was the haymow. By leaving the hayfork hanging and the original ladder intact, it is easy to share stories and showcase the original use of the main room, demonstrating how it was filled to the top with hay for the winter.

The original floor in this space was beautiful in its

own way. The years of use gave it so much character. It was impossible to keep it, as the boards were rough and uneven. I felt sorry about not keeping it, but Jim suggested we put down a soft pine floor and then distress it to look old. Hence, the Beat Up the Floor Party. We invited friends to come with tools, wear golf shoes with spikes, and be as creative as possible to make the new floor look old. Not only did we have fun, but the mission to give my barn's floor character was accomplished!

The lower level of my home was the original milking parlor. The original family milked twenty-six cows in that space. It had been left with stanchions hanging and feed bunks with old hay still in them. It was dark and rather frightening, with one light bulb hanging in the center of the space. All the walls were rock, and the three windows were shuttered. There were remains of raccoons and other small animals that had died in this space. There were two entrances for the cows and one pedestrian door on the east side of the building. This would certainly be the most challenging aspect of the project, especially since I had to create a living space there.

As we started brainstorming how to begin the remodeling, the only way to attack this space was to remove the entire lower east wall. The wood was in need of repair anyway, and with it open, we could start to clean the remains of approximately sixty years of milking residue. After removing the larger items and old hay, we began to power wash from top to bottom. The floor was slanted to the east, as all milking barns were, so the manure could be washed out easily. This helped in the cleaning process. After several power washings, we allowed it to dry thoroughly.

Now we were ready for designing the kitchen, bedroom and bath, and a casual sitting area. I give Jim Thompson all the credit for the lower level—other than my request to have as many windows as possible to look out over the pond while in my kitchen. It is a beautiful scene in every season.

It would be impossible to detail every move made to convert the barn to this pleasant place to live. The process took about eighteen months. The original beams were all left as they were. Jim created new beams only in places to hide electrical work and other wiring. You would never know they are not original.

The ceiling in the downstairs milking parlor is the original wood, and the joists, a structure used to frame an open space, are twelve inches apart rather than sixteen inches, which is more standard. I learned that from a farmer who was visiting. I was also able to determine that the barn was built in 1891, as an Amish man found it carved into the original rock foundation. He was interested in history and asked if he could examine the rock. Of course, I agreed, because I loved it when people showed interest in our projects. What a blessing to find it in the northeast corner of the rock foundation. It is not easy to see, but it is still there.

Living in the barn has been a wonderful experience. It has its idiosyncrasies, with a thirty-eight-foot ceiling and a rock lower level, but now Becky and Doug do not think it is a bad idea at all! My grandkids have had many sleepovers, and our family has so many memories of our weekly Sunday family dinners and holiday celebrations together as a family.

Bridge or No Bridge 1999

One of the things that impressed us as we drove into the property back in the early 70s was the Apple River running through the property. As you drove down the long lane, you came to the bridge that crossed over the river, and up the hill you went.

We learned that at one time, there was no bridge. The hired man that came to work for Mrs. Gabel would hear a bit of thunder, and no matter what he was doing, he would finish up quickly and head for home before the river rose and would not allow him to leave the property. The story goes that there was a bridge built that was less than desirable, so in 1960, Antonio Gabel had a bridge built. She had a relative who worked with a construction company of some kind, and they did the work. It seemed to be substantial—the keyword here being "seemed."

In early April 1999, the One Hundred Year Flood came to be a reality in Jo Daviess County. In April of that year, I received a call to the farmhouse at 4:00 a.m. from RJ Spillane. He said, "Go to the river. I don't think you will believe what you are about to see." So, as he said, I went to the river, and in no way would I have expected this to happen, but the bridge had been washed out.

It is very common for folks to have weather scanners to keep track of the storms that would pass through. So, RJ knew the flood was serious and had driven out to check on the bridge to find it washed away down the river.

That in itself was a big shock, as we knew this was the only way in and out of the farm. The river was very high and flooded the pasture that surrounded it as well. Looking at this river rushing and no bridge across it was surreal.

Years ago, the lane leading into the farm property had continued past the farmhouse and continued west up the hill to connect with Hodgin Road toward Apple Canyon Lake. At some point, the property became all farmland, and the road ceased to exist. We know very little about how, why that happened, or when exactly it happened.

With a newborn baby, the inability to leave the property became our main concern. All we could think of at this point was possibly getting permission to go up that hill through the neighbor's property to Hodgin Road, our only access to any public roads. This was extremely urgent, as baby Emma was due to get her two-week pediatric checkup. The neighbors were very open about us coming through the property but promptly reminded us that the ground was so saturated due to the flood that no vehicle could possibly drive up that hill. Yet another bump in the road!

A few days passed, and the land dried up enough for some sort of vehicle to transport Rebecca and Emma. With the help of a neighbor, it was decided we could use a four-wheel-drive tractor to pull a wagon holding Rebecca and Emma up the hill to a waiting vehicle, which would then take them to have the appointment. That method was successful, and we had to do that for some time as a plan for a temporary bridge was developed. A low spot in the river east of the bridge site was used by adding gravel and doing some excavating. Now the plan for a new permanent bridge was to begin.

Again, RJ Spillane to the rescue! He contacted engineers from around the area to evaluate the damage and discuss the possibilities of rebuilding. It was decided early on that the new bridge should be at least five feet higher than the one we had just lost. We then would have to raise the road on both approaching sides of the gravel lane to the bridge. This began to feel like we were buying another farm!

A more structured but still temporary bridge was put in while the work progressed on the road and new bridge. RJ was completely in charge, which put me at ease, carefully following the county requirements. By fall, we were accessing the farm over a higher, stronger, and more impressive structure.

The Farm Receives Publicity

As the barn was transformed into a beautiful living space, people in the community would stop by to see the progress. As mentioned before, the process took about eighteen months from start to finish. Once completed, *Galenian* magazine reached out to me and asked to interview me to publish an article about the barn. At this time, we had just started to have weddings on the property in the chapel, so the article discussed both the weddings and my new barn house.

In 2002, a mutual friend of mine from Lanark, Illinois, a small town about forty-five minutes from the farm connected me and the editor of the *Country Sampler*. My friend came every year to the Echoes of the Past event and visited the barn after it was finished. As she loved the barn house and rendition, my friend's interest really started the word of mouth traveling about what was being done at the farm. The editor came out to visit and get an overview of the project. She was very enthusiastic about the conversion and wanted to do an article for the magazine. This was followed up with pictures and stories and a pleasant time of putting the article together. Once the issue was ready for the newsstands, I was so excited and nervous. This was really "going public."

I was very satisfied with the whole publication and thoroughly enjoyed working with the crew from Country Sampler.

In 2005, High Noon Entertainment contacted the Galena Chamber of Commerce, asking about homeowners who had the vision to turn a nonresidence into a residence. From my involvement with the Convention and Visitors Bureau over the years, many people in Galena knew the story, and they referred the group to me. I was contacted by the *Rezoned* team, who explained they did the shooting and programming for episodes on HGTV. Could they come and see if the barn house renovation fit what they normally aired on their channel? A mix of emotions waved over me: there was excitement about actually being on HGTV, such exposure, and whether that was good, and I wondered, was this really worthy of a television show?

Before any personal interview, the company sent me a detailed questionnaire. The questions ranged from who I was (country girl versus city girl) to what animals were on the farm and whether I'd ever had second thoughts about the project. The big question that was very easy to answer was, "Why did you think this building could become a home?"

The barn had always seemed to capture both Dewey and me as an amazing structure that had strength and beauty even when it needed a new roof. The fact that Dewey grew up on a farm added to the reality of exactly what had happened in this barn for so many years. Cows were milked in the lower level. Actually, twenty-six cows could be brought in and placed to be milked. The upper level of the barn was a haymow to feed the cattle throughout the winter.

This was followed by a visit from a crew for photos and interviews—including interviewing Jim Thompson, of course. All four of my grandchildren were able to be a part of it, baking and climbing on an old ladder we kept for an authentic look. It was very exciting!

All this, together with pictures of the past, intrigued the crew from High Noon. So, the project continued, and the crew came to film. The episode was finished and released in July 2006 in a *Rezoned* episode.

They did an amazing job, and we are so comfortable with the results.

My Amazing Life

As we journey through life, we have no idea what the future holds. Whether you are eight years old and curious, a teenager and much more apprehensive, or a young adult with plans that you know will work out with determination and hard work, there is no way of knowing the path the journey will take you.

> That is because Man makes his plans (or women) and the Lord directs the steps.
> —Proverbs 16:9

How true that is, as I never knew I would end up living at a farm that I loved with a family right across the road. And my family it did become!

Over the years, I was able to love and welcome four beautiful grandkids into my life. Doug and Rebecca wanted plenty of kids to share their life with, and since then, it has been one of life's greatest joys.

Emma Brooke was introduced earlier when we discussed the bridge problem. Born on April 18, 1999, she was a typical first child: always seeming to be the most grown up even as a very young child. When she was an infant, I was living in the farmhouse with Becky and Doug while my barn house was being finished. I had the pleasure of feeding her bottles and rocking her to sleep and watching her change and grow daily. She was a very agreeable baby, making the first child quite a joy.

There were so many adjustments to be made in that year going into 2000. I started moving into the barn house, and Becky and Doug were busy making the farmhouse a home of their own. They were going through everything that first-time parents go through. As we moved ahead, I was presented with the news there would be another baby coming in August 2000. How exciting that now there would be a sibling—and fairly close in age! Suddenly, we were into more planning for a second child.

Anna Dorothy was born on August 24, 2000, and joined the family in a much more peaceful way, with the intact bridge making it a little easier to get to the hospital for appointments. How could a woman be more blessed than to be right across the road and be able to help but also walk home and leave the family to themselves!

Emma loved Anna from the start. Curious and always interested in whatever was happening, Emma was always right there. It was a busy household, and we were just beginning to have inquiries about holding weddings on the property—the first one being between Scott Byrne and his wife, Melissa.

Seeing the two of these girls develop was so much fun. They were quite different in personality. Anna had a personality that bubbled over with laughter and giggles. Emma was more stoic and serious. Yet they were best buddies. We bought a kid-sized John Deer Gator that Emma would drive with Anna beside her, and all over the farm they would go. They took dance and tap lessons together, and one of my favorite pictures is the two of them in their outfits. It seemed there was not a lot they did not do together. As we were transitioning to a new stage of life, we were blessed with child number three a couple of years later.

Matthew Duane was born on September 17, 2002. Now the household became an even busier one. Matthew had so much attention from his mom, dad, sisters, and grandmother. He was one lucky boy and the only one at that. It was especially fortunate that I could fill in at times to help out but even more fortunate that I got to know these children on a personal level. The girls could come over to the barn house for sleepovers and bake cookies, which happened weekly. Now there were more weddings on the weekends, so Becky and Doug were more heavily involved in that as well as parenting. However, that just meant more time for me to spend with the grandkids.

Matthew had a big smile with a twinkle in his eye right from the start. His personality actually reminded me a great deal of my late husband, Dewey. He was a big hit with his sisters, and before long, he had all of us wrapped around his little fingers. He was all boy, but he fit right in, baking cookies, baking bread, or doing whatever was going on. So the family was complete with two girls and a boy. Perfect!

Here comes another one of life's surprises! We were presented with news that there would be one more baby, expected in April 2004. In one way, this did not surprise me too much. Becky had always loved being friends with those who had large family gatherings. She had a good friend with an Italian background, and she loved being a part of their holiday parties with such celebration. Our own family was limited to a few cousins, and some did not live close to us. So, Claire Marie was born on April 27, 2004.

Can a baby be serious? Claire was! We could not get Claire to smile very often, even though she was happy and satisfied. She observed all the activity around her as though she were taking mental notes. We worked on getting her to laugh and be silly, and eventually, she did loosen up. Now she has the most beautiful personality, with such gracious ways of dealing with everyone around her. So, do you see how I feel about being so incredibly fortunate to live across the road and see these four wonderful children grow up?

As the years went by, Becky and Doug always planned an annual family picture. There are so many wonderful places on the farm that are great photo opportunities. We took pictures for Christmas cards and took pictures in different seasons for ongoing scrapbooks. It's wonderful to have a yearly picture history of the family and to see how they change as the years go by.

I have spoken so much about our family but must include my son-in-law's family, as they have been a critical part of this amazing journey. Jan and Ed live in DeRuyter, New York, where Doug grew up. Doug's sister, Melissa, and her family, as well as his brother, Mike, and his family are all in the same area. We have had the privilege of visiting them and his grandmother Dorothy, as well as aunts and uncles. On various occasions, Doug and Becky and the children have spent the week after Christmas through New Year's Day in New York. During a period when extra help was welcomed, Jan was here, and what a blessing that was. She and I became very close during that time.

A friend of mine told me about an idea she had when her grandchildren were young. As they came upon their tenth birthday, she took them on a trip of their choice. I loved that thought and decided to put that into play. Of course, Emma was the first, and she chose Washington, DC, as her destination. After some thought, I decided to take a sibling of their choice along, letting them pick who that would be.

Also, being a bit apprehensive, I decided to ask my sister to accompany us. My sweet sister, Mary, did not have any grandchildren, and she adopted mine in a loving way. So, Emma asked Anna to go to Washington, and we had a wonderful time. I was happy that it was the four of us together. It was fun for the girls, and it was fun for Mary and me.

When Anna turned ten, she wanted to go to New York City. She asked Emma to be her traveling companion, and I again asked Mary to go along as well. Again, a wonderful trip, with so many memories. A very funny part of that trip was trying to get Anna's ears pierced. She was determined to have them pierced in New York. We did not realize that a parent had to sign for the procedure. When asked, we were honest and said we were aunt and grandmother. No good! We left that shop and went on with our day. Anna was feeling so bad that my sister Mary decided we would go back the next day, and if a different person was working, Mary would be Anna's mom! So, she went along with the story she had a baby late in life. Who would know? It worked, and the ears were pierced in New York City, as Anna had wanted.

Now, it was Matthew's turn. I thought it would be nice if he could go with both grandmothers. I asked Jan about it, and she was very willing to join us going to Nashville! It was a double celebration, as the K-Love Christian Celebration was going on while we were there. Featured at this special occasion was *Duck Dynasty* (remember them?). Matthew was really into that show, and we were going to have the thrill of meeting them face to face. We divided our time between the concert events and downtown Nashville. We had pictures taken with the *Duck Dynasty* individuals, and it was such a wonderful time! And, oh, he asked Anna to go along. So far, Anna has been on every trip! This was a special time to share with Jan and the grandchildren. I am so grateful that Jan was with us in Nashville.

Then Claire turned ten. It seemed that everyone else had a destination in mind with no problem. Claire could not decide easily but did end up with Disney World, in Florida. I was a bit panicked, since I am not a fan of any kind of ride. She asked Anna to go along, and I knew we would be OK when it came time for the rides. The three of us went this time and had a great time. The weather was perfect, and I spent a lot of time on the benches while the girls rode the rides. And, yes, Anna was on every ten-year-old trip! I had the kids write a daily journal of the trip, and it is such fun to look back and recall the experiences.

As this book is written, they all seem so grown up. Emma is a senior in college and Anna a junior, both at the University of Illinois in Champaign-Urbana. They both had internships this summer navigating around the COVID-19 pandemic. Matthew will be a senior in high school and Claire a junior. We are not certain what this year will bring as far as classroom versus e-learning. It is a different kind of world right now.

However, this too shall pass, and they will go on with healthy, happy, successful lives. I am so thankful they grew up here in the country and had access to Chicago and other cities as they traveled with their parents. I am and always will be especially thankful that I lived across the road!

A life well-lived captures emotion and memories. Stories will always follow, and I believe that my daughter can bring light to the farm as well. It is a huge part of her life and her family's. A life full of love, explained by Rebecca.

Rebecca Riedl, Sandra's daughter

I met Doug in February 1994 in the lower lobby of the Ritz-Carlton Hotel, in Chicago. I was serving as the manager of Water Tower Place Parking, which also handled the valet service for the Ritz, and Doug had just been hired as a greeter (the guy who says hello to every guest arriving at the hotel). I swear, the minute I met Doug, my heart dropped, and I had butterflies in my stomach. No lie. He smiled at me, and I was head over heels. I don't even believe in stories like this! Fast-forward to May, and after many nights out with other employees at Bottoms Up (a local bar on State Street), we had our first date at an Italian restaurant on Rush Street. We sat outside and ate pasta. That was the beginning of our Chicago adventure. We spent that entire summer soaking up the city. We hit every neighborhood we could think of, going to blues bars and tons of restaurants. The first "I love you" was on the midnight blues cruise with a young singer who just belted out the blues. We fell in love fast and hard. It was the best summer of my life.

That fall, I moved downtown with a college friend, and Doug moved out of the corner of his Lake Shore Drive apartment (yes, he slept on an egg crate foam pad in the corner of a lakefront apartment for six months!) into a hellhole infested with roaches. That lasted less than a month, and he and Mark moved to Wrigleyville, not far from Kelly and me. That December, we bought two puppies—Jake and Fletcher—even though neither of our apartments allowed pets. The next fall, in September 1995, Doug and I rented an apartment together just a bit further west, at 3710 N. Leavitt. We had great landlords who also loved dogs. I began my MBA program at Loyola, and life was good.

In October 1995, Doug and I went to the farm for one night with the dogs. My parents were entertaining my dad's college friends. We all went to dinner at a local Italian restaurant in Galena, where we ate, drank, and laughed. The next morning, we awoke to find out something terrible had happened overnight: my mom had taken my father directly to Northwestern Memorial Hospital due to severe pain in his lower back. Forty-eight hours later, the diagnosis: lung cancer that had spread to the adrenal glands, and one had burst. Life was never the same again. Exactly four (very rough) months later, Duane E. Wolfram passed away in hospice with Gigi and me right there with him on February 23, 1996. Sixty-one years too young.

Fast-forward another year (during which time the church was acquired and moved here, a second celebration of life was held, and grad school was completed). On Memorial Day weekend 1997, Doug and I planned to watch the sunrise together up on the hill overlooking the farm. We took the 1979 red-and-white Chevy up there with coffee, and just as the sun peeked over the horizon, Doug dropped to one knee and proposed! I was so excited and overwhelmed I jumped off the tailgate to hug and kiss him but forgot to actually answer the question. Needless to say, it was a *yes*!

The wedding planning began soon after, and we chose a date of June 27, 1998. We were thrilled to have our own church on site to have the ceremony, and we planned a tented reception on the farm. The days leading up to the wedding were *crazy*, to say the least. Tons of small and large projects had to be completed, and the moment anyone took a break, Sandy would say, "Are you looking for something to do?" That became a running joke for years to come. Mike, Doug's brother, came out for a week to build the walking bridge to the church, and it is still a hit with brides twenty-two years later.

The day of the wedding arrived, and it was *hot*, probably the hottest day I've ever experienced. I remember waking up at 7:00 a.m. that morning (after a very late night at the rehearsal and dinner), and it was already eighty-five degrees. I walked outside, and Gigi was in the garden, touching up one last area. The whole farm was busy the entire day, and just before the ceremony was set to begin, my lovely Aunt Mary, always so helpful, changed a load of laundry. Just as she started the dryer, the power went out— not just in the house but on the *entire farm*. There we were, with 220 guests showing up in 105-degree heat, plus humidity, and there was no power for the church, band, caterer, or anything. Nobody wanted to tell me what was happening, but it didn't take long to figure out. Somehow, by the grace of God, neighbors brought over some generators, and we pulled off an incredibly beautiful and fun wedding day. Just as Doug and I were about to leave in the Model A at 11:00 p.m., a *huge* storm rolled in, and we made it to the end of the road just as the lightning, thunder, and rain took over. We made it to our bed and breakfast (a silo in Hazel Green), looking forward to some air-conditioning and a hot tub, but as we sipped drinks, waiting to jump in, we realized the hot water heater wasn't working and the water was ice cold. What a day!

What happened next? We were ready to start a family! We knew we wanted a large family, and we were both ready to begin that journey. Soon I discovered I was pregnant, and our first baby was due in April. We also knew we wanted to move to the farm, and plans were in progress for Doug to move his financial business to Warren. I was going to continue to work for Standard Parking two days at home and one day in Chicago. Gigi decided to convert the hay barn into a home (Doug and I thought she was crazy!), and we sold our house in Des Plaines and moved all our belongings to the farmhouse a few weeks before the due date. I went into labor on a Sunday morning, and we made it back to Northwestern Memorial while counting labor pains the entire way. Emma Brooke Riedl joined the world at 5:17 p.m. on Sunday, April 18, 1999.

My career plans sounded great before Emma was born, but once she arrived, there was no way I was going to drive to the city every week, even if it was only for a day. During that summer, we had discussed career options, and a few people had inquired about getting married at our farm. That October, Galena held its first bridal show, and Doug encouraged me to sign up as a vendor. He created our very first website. I gathered photos from our own wedding, and off I went! I booked two weddings at that bridal show in Turner Hall! I remember that Doug, Sandy, and Emma came to see me there, and we were so excited. This era was the very beginning of wedding venues becoming popular. No one had heard of barn weddings, and the craze for outdoor events and venues other than banquet halls had not yet begun. As they say, timing is everything! Also in that first year, Doug joined Citizens State Bank as an investment executive, and he has been there ever since.

The year 2000 marked the beginning of Oak Hill Weddings, and Anna Dorothy became a part of our life in August. We started slowly with the business—just ceremonies at first, then a few cocktail hours and receptions started in 2002. We were all hands on deck in those early years. We recruited friends to help us, but it was mostly Sandy, Doug, and myself. We all would set up and clean up; Sandy was the officiant, I was the planner, and Doug drove the Model A or horse carriage and bartended. In 2002, Matthew entered the picture, and Claire, our caboose, was born in 2004.

As the business grew, we recruited people from our local community to help us with the operations. Doug phased out of bartending to be with the kids, and I continued to work every event from start to finish (exhausting!). We were getting busier every year, and by 2010, every Saturday was booked and quite a few Fridays. In 2011, we poured a concrete pad (no more lost sleep worrying about wet, muddy grass!), and in 2012, we bought our own tent. We added lights to the pine trees and created a few outdoor ceremony locations (Barnhouse lawn, Twin Oaks, and the Path of Pines). By 2014, we had put on more than fifty events in our six-month season.

You know that saying, "Something's gotta give"? Well, that something was a wake-up call in the form of a breast cancer diagnosis in September 2014. That same month, Matthew was diagnosed with Chiari malformation. Both of us needed to have a major surgery. I immediately had to step away, but this was a blessing in disguise. We now had a full setup and cleanup crew and bartenders, and now we began scheduling managers for each event. I was lucky enough to just have a bilateral mastectomy with no chemo or radiation needed. Matthew had surgery ten days after me, and Grandma Jan saved us by coming to stay for a month while we recovered together in our new recliners, which we loved.

By spring 2015, I was healed enough to start the season again but with a different approach. I had full coverage for all the operational duties, and I focused on sales and management. This has been our process ever since, and it has made life so much better. The business has grown without very few bumps in the road (knock on wood). We did have one major issue: in December 2018, I called the county zoning office to discuss the possibility of a building permit for a pavilion, and we realized that we needed to acquire an updated special use permit. After plenty of lengthy phone calls and sleepless nights leading up to the county board meeting, at which the fate of the business would be determined, all worked out and Oak Hill was back to business as usual.

In 2019, we added the Woodland Forest ceremony location, a "real" gravel parking lot, and decided to bite the bullet and build a pavilion. The building permit was issued, and construction began in late November 2019. We were *so* excited (as were all our 2020 brides!) to begin the next season with a brand new all-white wooden pavilion, with gutters (perhaps the most exciting part to me!), chandeliers, string lights, and windows to the east and west. So, what happened next? I'm sure you know. COVID happened, and we came to a grinding halt: forty weddings rescheduled and six cancelled. Talk about tears and stress—just wow. However, here I am, on August 18, 2020, and we are still a business. And for the future? We are staying hopeful and taking each day with gratitude as we continue to navigate through this time. We will survive this, and as I always say, it could be worse. I have so much love for the farm and for our family. Our business is a labor of love, and I couldn't be happier that we are all a part of how it grew into such a successful venture. My dad, Dewey, would have been proud! The love story is truly living on.

So, as I was hoping the farm would be ours and dealing with the unknown, I had said that if God granted us the privilege of having the farm, I would share it with everyone.

At that time, I was thinking of all family and friends. Now thousands of people have come here as wedding guests, brides, and grooms, as well as all the other side events that come up. It has been such a privilege to share, and I give all the glory to God!

Love in Its Present Form

As I mentioned earlier, we never know just what the future brings. We make our plans, and the Lord directs our steps. This book might never have been written if it had not been for the 2020 COVID-19 pandemic creating more time on everyone's hands. Also, in what ended up being a blessing, everyone was under one roof again, which had not happened in some time.

Emma had been in Australia since January 2020, studying in Sydney. Fortunately, the entire family planned a trip to visit her and travel the country in early March, right before the stay-at-home mandate and travel bans were placed. They were able to spend that time freely traveling in Australia and return home right before the shutdown was put into effect. Emma's time in Australia was then cut short, as she had to return home in March as well. Anna and Matthew and Claire were all homebound, as well.

Fortunately, Anna had an internship in a Chicago suburb, and she was able to work with them online for several weeks. They then allowed her to participate in the office in the later spring and the rest of the summer.

Matthew was fortunate to be asked to be a part of a construction crew. This was something he had never done before, but with his versatile personality, he could easily adapt. He had always had a lot of chores to do around the farm and was young and strong.

Claire had lined up a job as a lifeguard, and then the pools were closed. She was then asked to babysit for a local couple but declined due to the lifeguard position that was still up in the air. Upon letting them know that she would not be lifeguarding, they happily employed her.

For some time before this, my daughter had been encouraging me to write down stories about the farm and some favorite memories. I had attempted to do that, but I never really had a plan or idea about where to start. With time on her hands, Emma approached me and suggested we write a book about the farm. We had to stay away from everything and everyone as much as possible, so what better activity than to sit down together and gather thoughts. So she became my coach and my editor!

It has been a wonderful experience to look back and review what Dewey and I did together. I have now been a widow for twenty-four years, left with love's greatest memories. We were married for thirty years, so that time frame is interesting. I have been blessed in those twenty-four years so richly with family and friends and good health.

I was given a small plaque with this verse from Jeremiah 29:11: "For I know the plans I have for you declares the

Lord, plans to prosper you, and not to harm you, plans to give you hope and a future." This verse has reflected a lot of truth in my life and the uncertainties for which one cannot plan.

There is another verse that I cannot live without, and that is Proverbs 3:5: "Trust in the Lord with all your heart and lean not on your own understanding. Acknowledge Him in all you do and He will make your paths straight."

What is next? People always ask that question. No more buildings will be moved as far as I can see. We have the beautiful church, with its history, and the fun schoolhouse as well. Most recently the little old woodshed has become a fun new cocktail bar, and Becky has a brand-new pavilion for wedding receptions that catches the lighting of the most beautiful sunsets. But who knows? Perhaps if I don't see a new venture, it doesn't mean that Doug and Becky or even a grandchild might not have some ideas!

Today, Emma and Anna are both attending the University of Illinois at Champaign. Emma will graduate in the spring of 2021 and with a constant urge to travel, I hope she continues to write wherever she may be before she starts navigating her post graduate life in Chicago. Anna, a girl with overflowing passion in everything she does, is a junior in the Gies College of Business and continues to pursue her artistic abilities.

Matthew is a senior in high school and plans to study engineering, although the college has not been formally decided. He is thinking of Colorado, but we cannot stand the thought of him being so far away. He is a great kid. And Claire is a junior this year. She was an avid gymnast and is now into volleyball, which we will play once the COVID-19 pandemic is over. Recently, she has been playing golf with the high school golf team. She is a good athlete, no matter the sport.

Becky and Doug are constantly busy with their careers, involving weddings and Doug's financial business. At this point in life, it will be difficult to get everyone together for family vacations as they used to annually. Doug and Becky will have to plan their special time away.

As for myself, I am planning to be what they call "farm manager" for a long time. I love taking care of the gardens, my two donkeys, the multitude of farm cats, and a few chickens. I wanted to live on the farm from the first day I saw it in the early seventies. It has been a dream come true! That is the beauty of the farm. The love will live on, and the ideas will continue. My husband is buried at home, as I will be, and the family will continue the love affair.